Looking Inside My Soul

By Alf Jackdaw

About me

I am using the pen name Alf Jackdaw as I do not want people to know my identity. I am an average man living in an average town, living on an average housing estate.

I am an amateur poet and phone photographer. I have created this book for myself. I wanted to collate some of my work.

I have taken great comfort and solace in these photos and words during troubled times. If one other person enjoys, takes comfort or solace in these words, the effort I have put into creating this small book would have been worth it.

Thanks!

These poems and photos have been written/taken over many years, from boy to man. I have taken, written, edited and published this book. I am an amateur and I've never done this before. I apologise for creating an unpolished book and for any mistakes.

Thanks

When

When you are beaten and down
Broken and can only manage a frown
When you are enveloped in grief
Unable to receive any relief

When you've lost something you hold dear
There is nothing left but the fear
When you're lost and hurt unable to cry
There is nothing left inside to try

When all the hope is too far gone
And nothing left for you to rely on
When eventually the sun rises again
will it remove the heaviest stain

Wights

The divine isle of the wights
Terrifying spirits cause frights
Sacred roaming on all nights
Feel the spirits until morning lights
Assailed by the Cyning Wihtwara
With the gods brawn and guile
The land blessed, mild and fertile
Wights, hard to please and hostile
spirits of land will task you with trial
Paradise, beware of the wights of the Isle

Lessons

God has tried to teach me the lessons, over time I have made my
confessions

I've lent to far away to repent, I've followed all my evil crimes
through with evil intent

I drift tried and alone, a grave rift between, I've seen too much
where ever I've been

Suffer

Scratching and scribblings of a mad man
Awful confused thoughts written on paper
Need to erase frantically with a scraper
Must cover up the man's contemplation
Ashamed for the world to see the situation

Truth hidden to save the embarrassment
The man should openly show impediment
Everything covered up to save the blushes
The problem of the man should be shown
So we can make sure no one suffers alone

Circling

Two in the morning, the thoughts come knocking
The bleak, raw sentiments start flocking
My chest tightens with some pain
Body temperature has risen, is my mind sane?
The repetitive sequence of my night
Is my defective, debilitated mind in full fright?
The black dog is prospering here and the wolves are circling near
I am struggling to live with the fear
I consequently, persistently let fall a tear
Why am I unable to cope? No energy left to hope

Crave

Glass hearts waiting to be broken
Dreams deep, too far down they've sunken
So gentle trying to avoid being smashed
Someone needs to break out
Lunge forward pave the way forward toward what we all crave
Instead of taking refuge in our mind's cave

Relax

I can hear my heartbeat deep in my ears
Continue to pound in my head, can't relax
This is my penance, my life's burdened tax
Relaxation and peaceful time greatly lacks
I feel the sick sitting in my throat and chest
I'm unable to achieve some appropriate rest
I wish I could have a safe place, like a nest
Trying to relax and sleep feels like a quest
Laying here alone, tired and confused
My pitiful mind exhausted and bruised
Piling on worry and doubt, this now fused
Brain doesn't grant slumber, sleep refused

Evening

Every tiring day arrives the cruel evening
Lay here in the bed staring at the ceiling
Trying my hardest to suppress the feeling
Tired, wired and lost, my mind is keeling
I am left unable to focus due to the pain
Leave the window open hoping for rain
Small comfort slowing the anxiety train
Cannot find the sentiment of peace again
Mind, soul and heart bursting of loneliness
I feel weak and pathetic, I must confess
These suffering thoughts make me less
Of a man, my head full of my past regrets
Creates shame, worry, and further frets
I am shattered, twisted and ashamed
To be this fragile, kind thoughts unclaimed
Not just past regrets, the worry is there
For present and future, wish i didn't care

End

An end to a alluring, gratifying day
Waves calmly swirling on the shore
The sea current acting like a claw
Recovering the land to the sea
This is how I want my world to be
Daylight faded to near darkness
Orange clouds holding the calmness
The last glimmer of day, sun now weak
The last of the angelic birds speak
Until the morning red sun reverbs
The citrus soft smells created by herbs
Being drawn in with each gentle breath
The apricot sun has now nearly gone
Leaving us with the last thereon
Sight of the intense dark green hills
The delicate soul, the horizon fulfils
Last embrace of the breath taking view
Until the sun introduces the morning new

Goodbye

I missed my opportunity to say goodbye
I frequently, often tell myself the lie
The text message I sent a few days before
Was enough effort made, yeah sure
Your passing left my heart on the floor

Recovery from pain was meant to be slow
It has been completely non existent, so no
I continue to feel nothing, essentially low
My fragile fragmented mind still in bits
My heart battered, bruised it's the pits

The time we had together was too short
But this was not either of our fault
I try to live by the lessons you taught
Support from you, never openly sought
Offered to me without a second thought

All the phone calls and time together
I will not forget you and our time, never
You did not know the ways you helped me
I felt blessed when I came round for tea
Your garden lovely, especially the fig tree

After your passing I don't know how to feel
My whole life ruptured, it's a broken wheel
I was deeply sorry you suffered your ordeal
Your nature was second to none, so gentile
We still come to see you, to you we kneel

In

My desired eagerness to try hard to fit in
I feel I need to lose weight and be thin
I keep a straight non committal face
So I can hide the fact I feel out of place
Growing up knowing I didn't conform
Most of the other people were the norm
Don't have the same interests as most did
I'm hiding my differences, don't lift the lid
I am worried, it's very lonely to not fit in
I hide away silently and take it on the chin
The horrible feelings and I couldn't be me
Keep yourself low and hidden was the key
I want something different from the others
My acting creates my formidable covers

Moor

The scraggy forcefulness of the moor
Feel the the vigour of the imposing Tor
beauty of nature crashes with man as one
The simple and sublime compare to none

An untamed and wild mural landscape
Offers solace and comfort to some
Offers bleakness and makes others numb
Jeopardy leaves the atmosphere grum

The moor has stolen my heart and soul
When I am far remote it takes its toll
There is beauty within the savage climate
Rocks telling a story of the moor's fate

Stones and slag heaps laying around
Man has drained, ravaged the ground
Makes me feel equally lost and found
Me and the terrain are now closely bound

Fight

To those who are lost, frightened and alone
There is someone willing to answer the phone
Be kind to yourself, others will come with the attacks
It is fine to show that your confidence lacks
Please do not feel ashamed and think this is weak
This shows a strength and you are very unique
To anyone tired and feeling extremely down
There will be future reasons to raise that frown
Keep going, fight like you can, you are strong
Time to step out and prove your doubters wrong
There is plenty of good times to follow from now
Fight now, never let go and throw in the towel
Never forget it's fine to feel lows and take the blows
Never give up. This is temporary, feeling the lows
I take the drugs and therapy, I won't become reliant
Temporary measures to help, I will remain defiant

Free?

Most people need to be free to roam
The fulfilment of a wander and comb
A long ponder, what of the old places
Empty and cold with no familiar faces

Minority still yearning for the atchin tans
Huge, vast, the green landscape pans
Breathe in, the smell of cut grass fades
A way of life, threaten for decades

Kin together, sitting around the yog
In the light bavval and dense fog
The sight, the majority rarely seen
To think of the years that have been

The gorger never saw, we let them be
Now they all need to wake up and see
folk no longer in the clearings of the tree
These people can no longer be free

Vardos no longer spotted in the lane
The few trying to keep a way of live in vain
These people now hidden on council sites
Not allowed to be free, to soar like kites

Trees

The unnerving whistling shiver of the trees
Leaves spin, twisting in the raw breeze
Spirits at their worst, haunting won't ease
Try to get them on side, try to appease
Eerie at night in the woods, the unease
This is what you cannot see's diocese
The dread surrounds you like a disease
Spirits have their plan, pay their fees
To harmlessly navigate though the trees
Life in these woods is the clear absentees
New noise, woods have their one sneeze
All sins are clear, the thick woods sees
what you are, these woods will tease
Torture of the spirits have me on my knees

View

The astounding view from the cliff of a another land
I have a longing for this place I don't understand
The panorama is exclusively visible on a clear day
Only the distance I need to travel keeps me away
The sun flashes specs of light off the sparkling sea
The wonder of the view is appreciated not only by me
Land on the other side of the sea looks a healthy green
The opposite side of the water I have never been
Our castle stands proud on the mighty white cliff top
I wonder if the people on the other side like our backdrop

Trapped

Overbearing suffocation of being trapped
The enjoyment for this life untapped
My tragic path has already been mapped
My potential gone, it has been capped
By the others who chose not to adapt

Contradicting treatment of my feelings
Searching heart and soul for meanings
Unable to free myself, can't start to leave
Rest bite to the mundane, I would receive
They cannot see, they are extremely naive

Loss

Exhilarating feeling you get when trying for a baby
Hear the words I'm pregnant, thirteen weeks later the baby is no
more
Our baby who never came into our world was not a person by law
The tragic loss, no one else saw
My feelings after this, I was expected to withdraw
Our baby had no flaw, not exposed to the world remains untainted
heretofore
The loss, we could have never foresaw
How do you act and feel? the emotion raw
These losses are not about the man, the woman's feelings come
before
Outpouring of grief not allowed, life had crumbled to the floor

Fool

I am a immense fool
My own sanity too cruel
I have tried to cure pain
My efforts are always in vain
Please be gentle and kind
The anguish from a disturbed mind

I want to go to leave
I am whom that shall not achieve
I am lost and confused
My mind is left very abused
Are my thoughts tormented
Memories worn and demented

I'm a struggling fool
The way I treat people is cruel
I've caused a lot of pain
Tried to be me, failed in vain
I'm sensitive not kind
This nastiness is in my mind

Light

Please give me your light
You've left my heart in mid flight
I can't be too far out of your sight
You continue to give me your fight
Your determination as always is
A revelation to me, I'm so glad
That you've never left me to be free
When I'm with you I can truly be me
You always fulfil my complicated need
Thanks for continuing to lead

Losing

Losing you has resulted in a emptied space
Which I struggle to face
My feelings get worse, as I am no longer sure
I have no clue
Whether I have truly and completely misplaced you
All I have is a torn heart that truly aches
I have made too many mistakes

Christmas

The sweet smell of roasting parsnips
Thoughts of the taste tingling the lips
The fresh fragrance of the noble fir
Gives the mind an exciting powerful stir
Turkey slowly turning golden brown
Candle light sparkling and blinking
Starts the excited mind thinking
The glittering gold round baubles
Takes your thoughts far away
From the bone chilling cold outside
A large bowl of Satsuma's and walnuts
Sitting by the bucket of coal waiting
To be dashed onto the smouldering fire
Greetings cards dangling from wire
Carols being sung by a frozen choir

Clouds

Cloud formations have made me feel the elations
Tint of orange, puffy white with hint of yellow
Helps one find solace, makes the mind mellow
Observing clouds keeps away feelings of low
I have realised the beauty of the clouds now
Beautiful colours from the sun, clouds will allow

Town

The town built in the valley of the Ouse
We only hear and read the bad news
This has created the bad reputation views
People that cannot see beyond this lose

Town has plenty of eye catching buildings
Steeped in history and legendary stories
Unfortunately, currently full of the tories
Set on the King's Cross line for our ease

Surrounded by the river, trees and fields
Local farmers work hard for their yields
Encircled by sensational walking routes
I use a medieval bridge for my commutes

Season

My heart filled with the joys of the season
Trepidation, finally a reason!
Darkness and cold of winter left behind
The suns gentle caress, mild and kind
Trees budding green, flower petals peaking
Out of the soft grass, the colours leaking
Came out from the drying, lush fruitful ground
Every season ends, now time for spring's round

Bright

Bitter sweet end of day
Still bright, in bed I Lay
Unable to leave my bed
Due to weakness, less said

The sun glows red, still bright
I could be in the light
Wish what is ailing me
Would leave, I would be free

Sun sinks, distance glimmer
The light still grows dimmer
Melancholy, the day ends
The darkness now descends

Our

Can you remember when we first met
My lust was trapped in your tight net
Our love initially, harshly barred
When I saw you I would tremble hard
We would hide our feelings to the world
Sneaking around while our hearts whirled
You were warned about me, told beware
We have remained strong, survived anywhere
Our working stopped us from having time
However our little time was sublime
We have built our lives from nowhere
Our fate not confirmed, up in the air

Fear

My chest pounding with fear
Heart rate fast changing gear
Hoping to end current mood
My thoughts in full on feud
How can this end for me
Can't wriggle my thoughts free
Stop the morning coming
Take tablets for numbing
Hiding in my dark room
Descending feel of doom
Forced to do things I can't
Need a self kindness grant
Tell yourself everything's fine
Are my thoughts still mine

Time

They say time is all we have got
Time twists and ties me in a knot
I have another chance this dawning
Let's fulfil aspirations this morning
Time moves with my fleeting feelings
Our youth is among time's stealings
Time marches inevitably
To our end intentionally
Time ends my failed hostile day
All that is left for me today
Is to hide myself far away

Blighty

Get me back to Blighty
My anxiety is making me flighty
I'm not sure if I'm tanned
Sunburnt, too hot in this land

Clock

Nature's golden rays endeavour to snatch the last peek
At the land before the dark clouds engulf the earth
The sun desperate for a gap to weep and duck through
I am desperately clutching onto the last of the day
It's conclusion nigh with every tick tock from a clock
Comparable to a flock of birds, the time is flying away

Lust

From the fatal first kiss
It's should not be like this
Temptation of the flesh
Should we run off, start afresh
This is not right
We continue to meet at night
Our partners need not know
We can meet on the low
We know this is not right
But feelings of delight
Are very strong
It is so so wrong
We shouldn't be meeting
Hopefully these feelings are fleeting

Sky

Crashing's of the fast waves
Lashing's from the sea spray
Dots of lights far away
Lots of stars in the sky
Shots of light, beautiful
In the lonely night sky
Skin tingles, joy came by

Rain

The rain pelting the window
Dark heavy clouds sitting low
Sound of the wind whipping past
The ferocious storm came fast
Old trees creaking they won't last
Drops of rain hitting the ground
Hops back up, heavy rain drops
Gales blasting, bang letter box
Consistently knocking door
Rattling you to the core
Afraid, I can't take much more
Wheelie bins losing their load
Debris flying down the road
I'm scared of extreme weather
At the end of my tether

Butterflies

I felt the butterflies
Helped me tell the strong lies
I thought my heart was gone
Hysteria, my soul feeds on
The excitement felt good
Laying together in bed
Awake all night, words unsaid
Limbs entwined bodies as one
Our love won't be undone
I feel giddy and warm
Swirling like a sandstorm
My heart feels very warm

Content

Pleasure of content
This is by what life is meant
Together lives spent

Mundane

My life is mundane
Boring driving me insane
Please challenge my brain

All

Everyday give your all
I wasted the day, the fool
Unable to stand tall

Birds

Bright sun has risen
Can hear birds, time to listen
My new tradition

Verge

I'm on the verge here
I have given all this year
My mind is unclear

Today

Today I am afraid
Today this won't be portrayed
My bad thoughts replayed

Photos

Dorset

Corfe castle summer's day

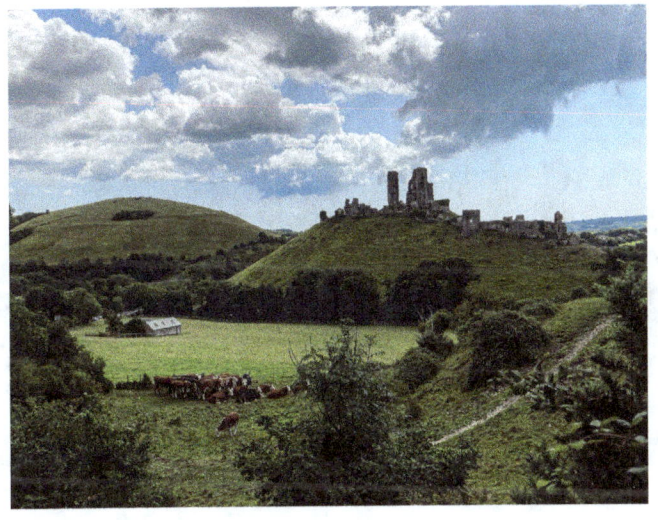

Devon

Warm autumn day in north Devon

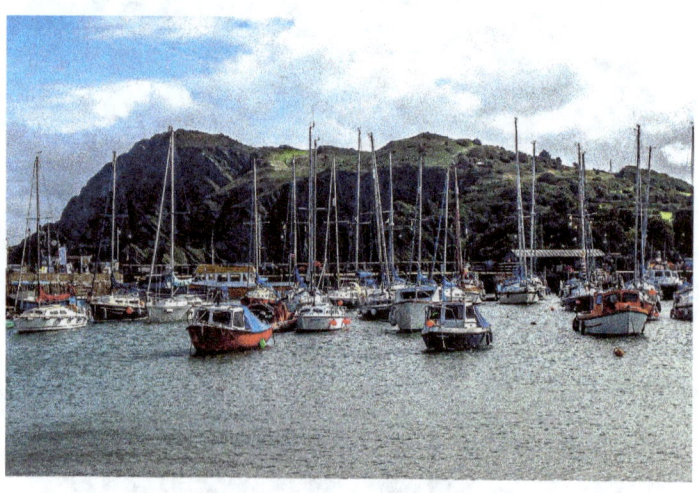

Dorset

Summer's day in Swanage

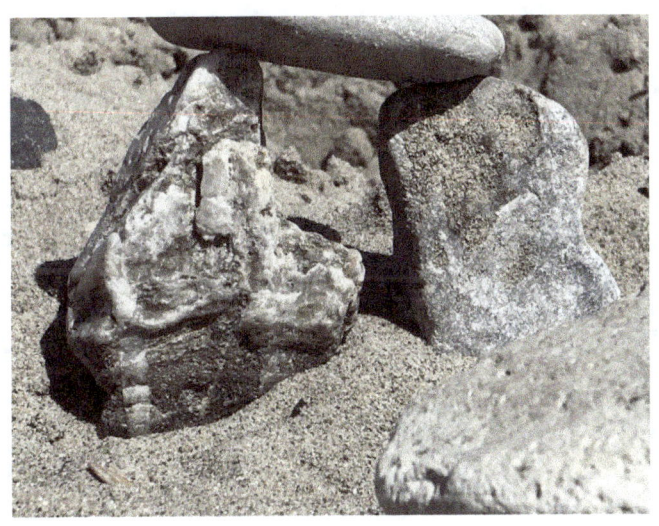

Bedfordshire

Snowy winter day in central Bedfordshire

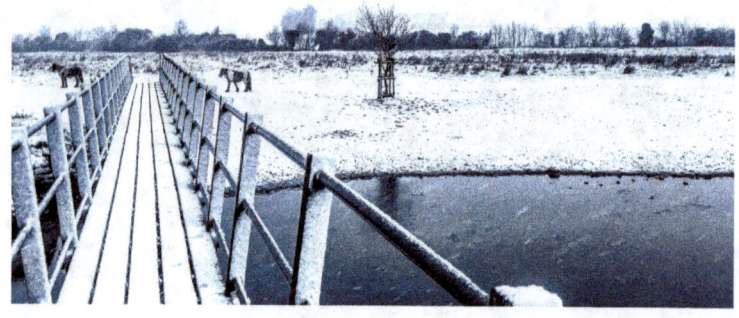

Cornwall

Warm winter's day in St Austell area

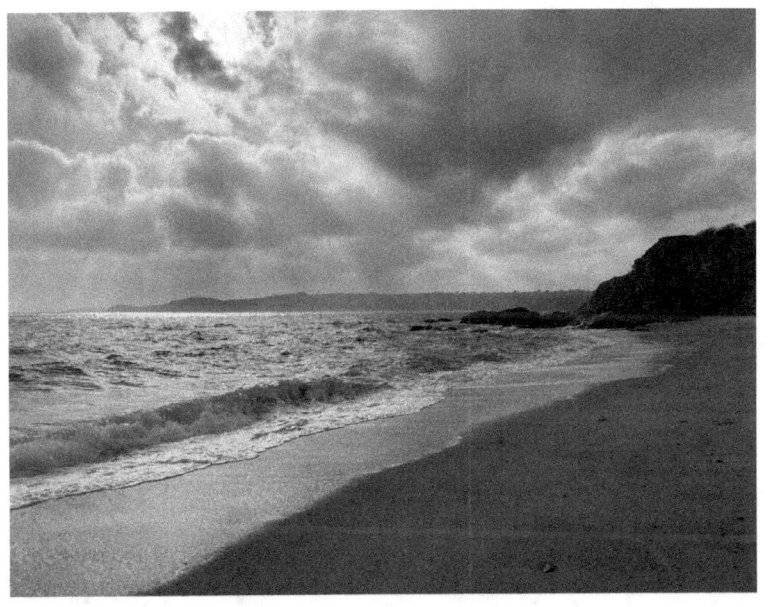

Cornwall

Hot autumn day in Rock

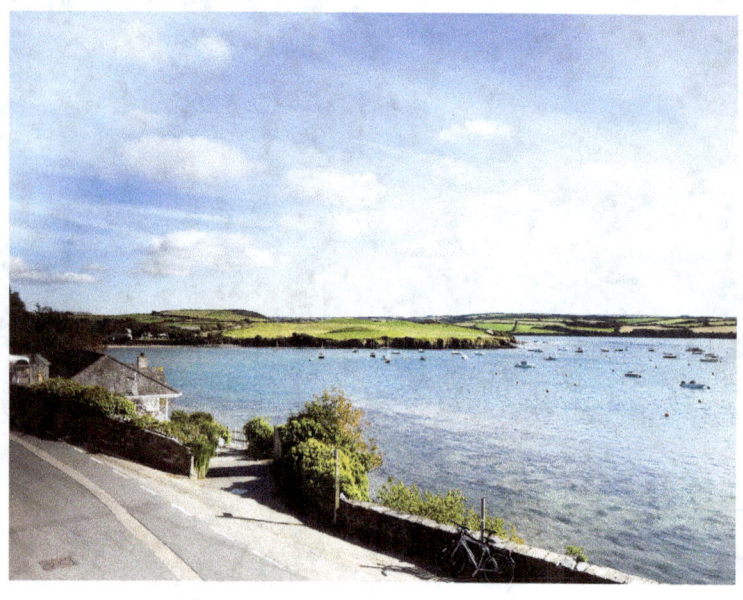

Cambridgeshire

Early morning in spring

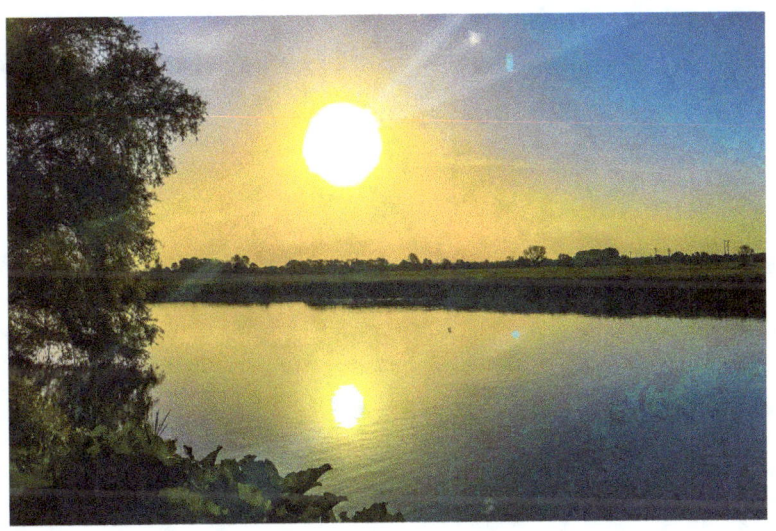

Cornwall

Autumn day in rock

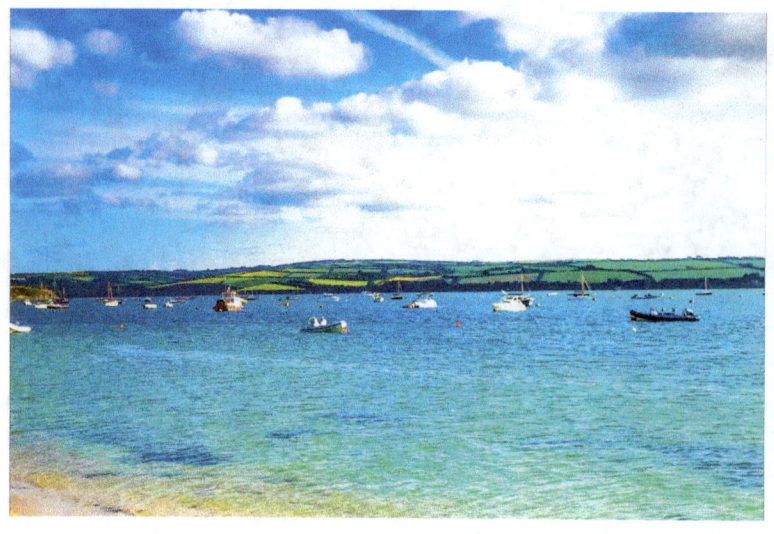

Dorset

Summer's day Durdle's Door

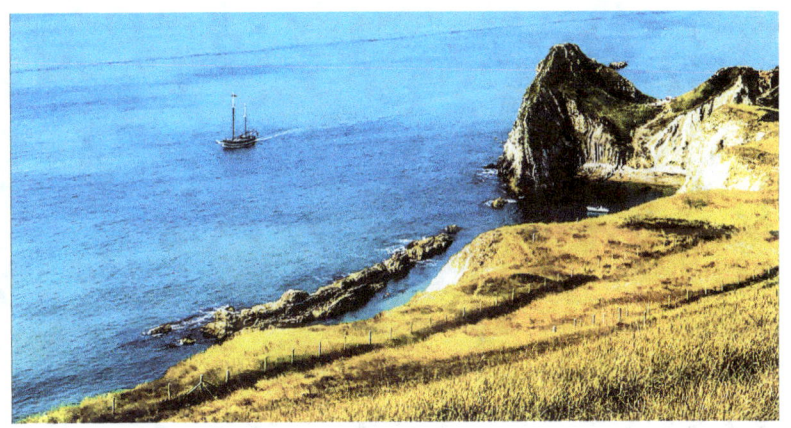

Dorset

Lulworth Cove

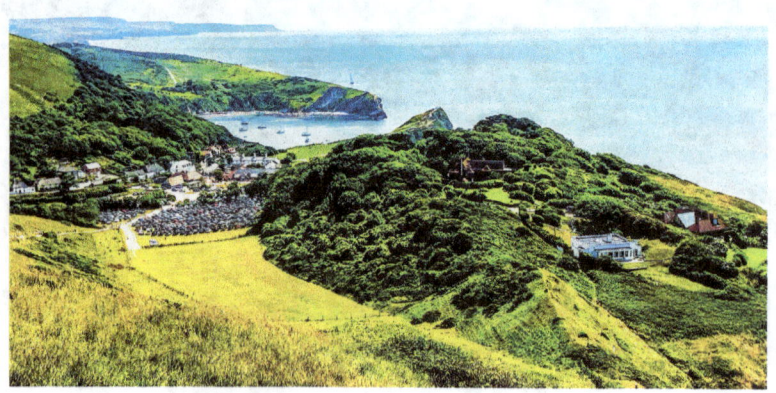

Bedfordshire

Early spring morning in central Bedfordshire

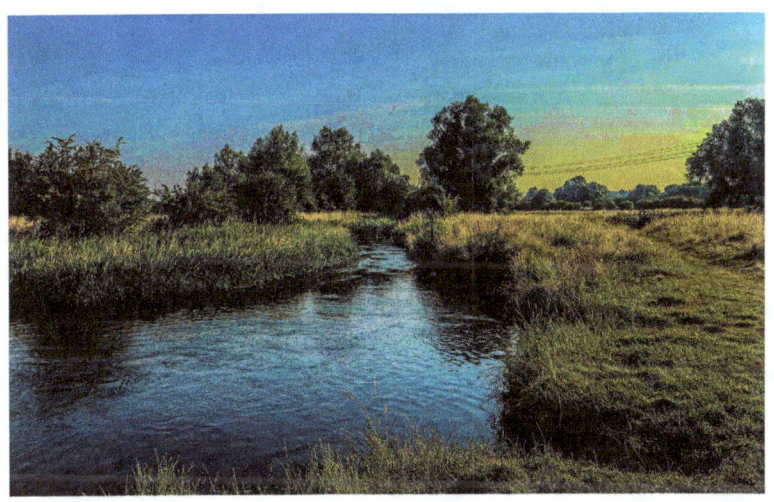

Bedfordshire

Poppies in a field

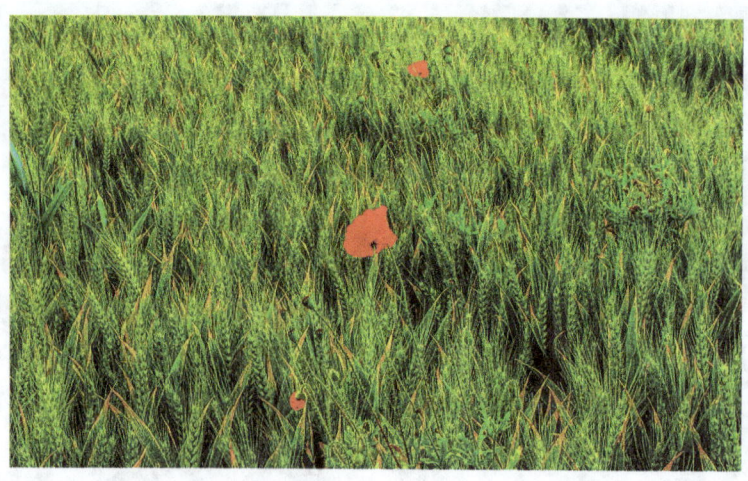

Cambridgeshire

Wet summer day

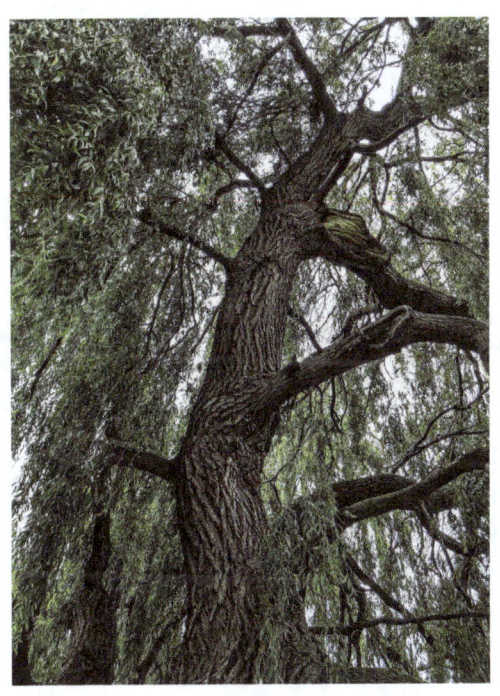

Bedfordshire

Sunrise central Bedfordshire

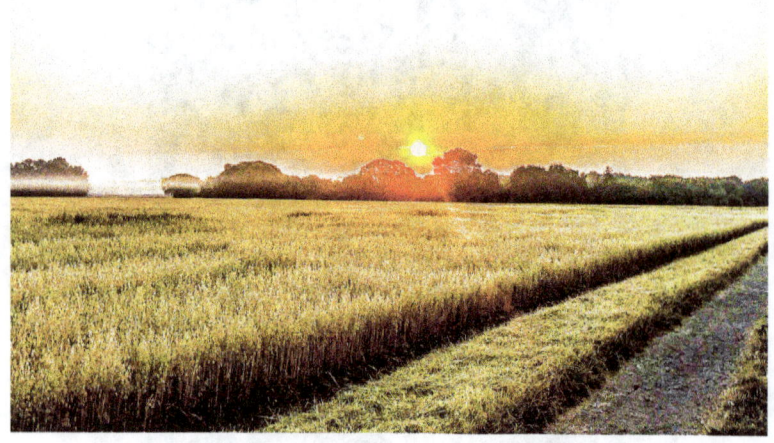

Dorset

Summer Durdle's Door

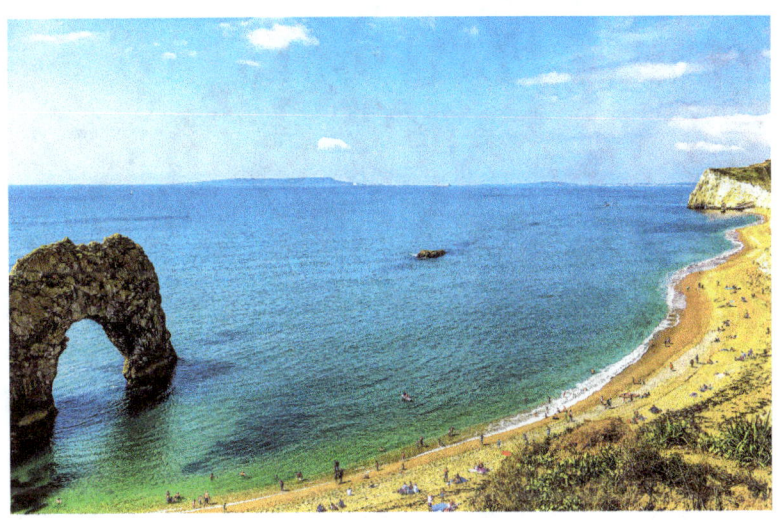

Cornwall

Autumn Tintagel

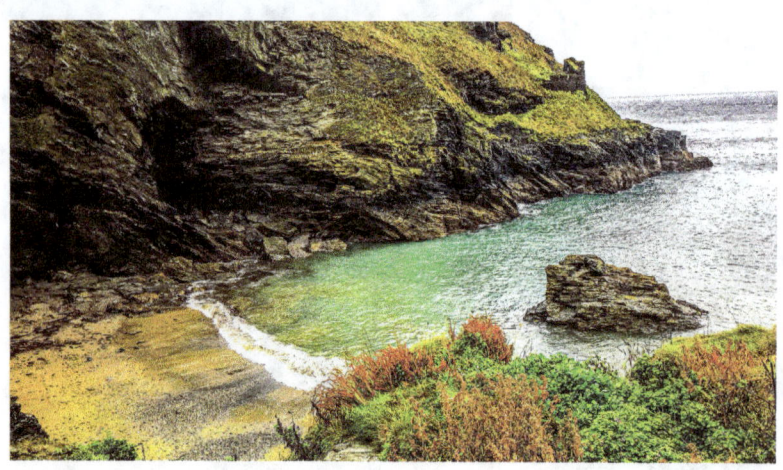

Cornwall

Rock in early autumn

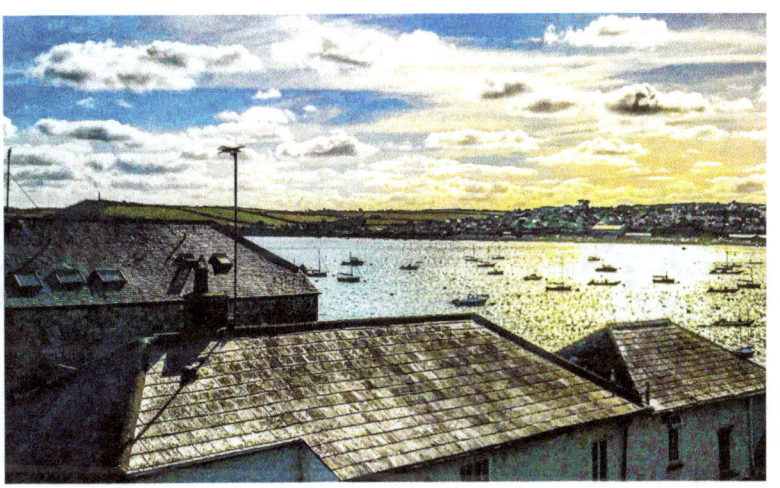

Bedfordshire

Summer in the fields

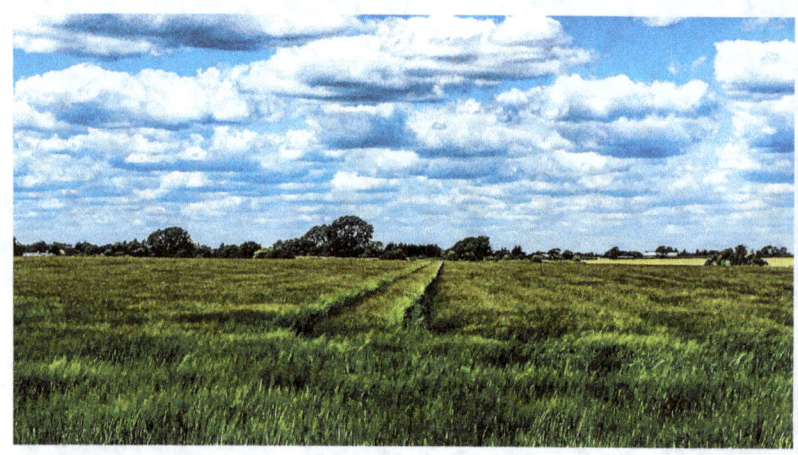

Bedfordshire

Poppies in summer

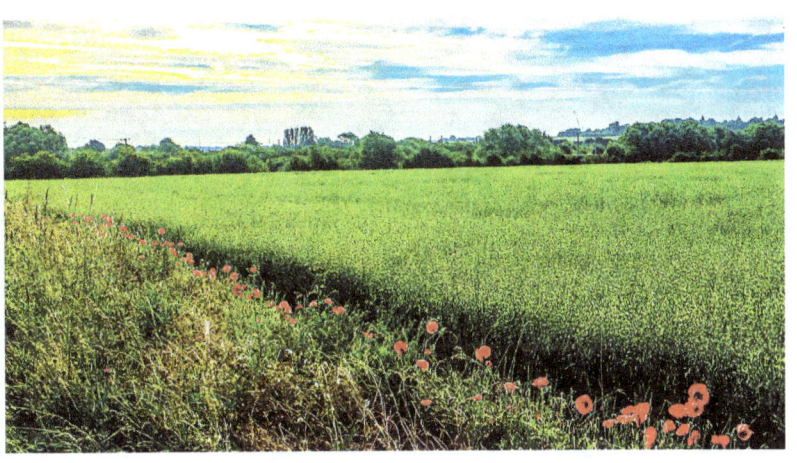

Cornwall

Cloudy autumn day at Tintagel

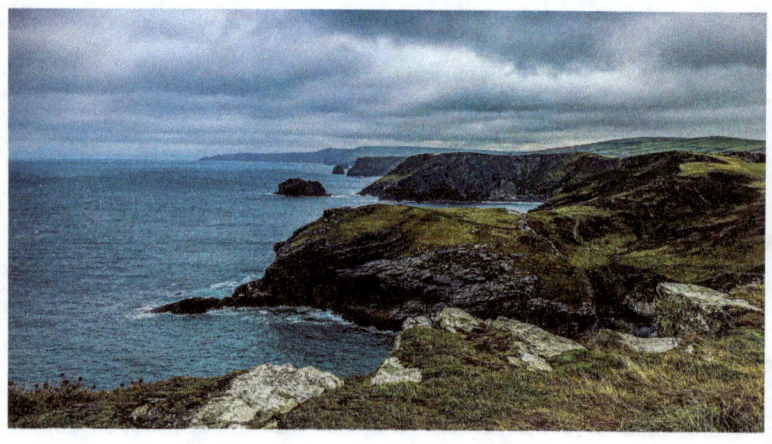

Bedfordshire

Sunrise in central Bedfordshire

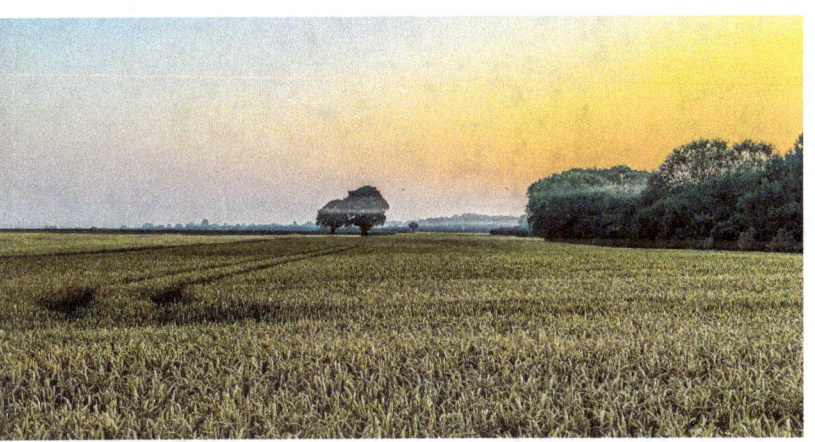

Dorset

Durdle's Door area

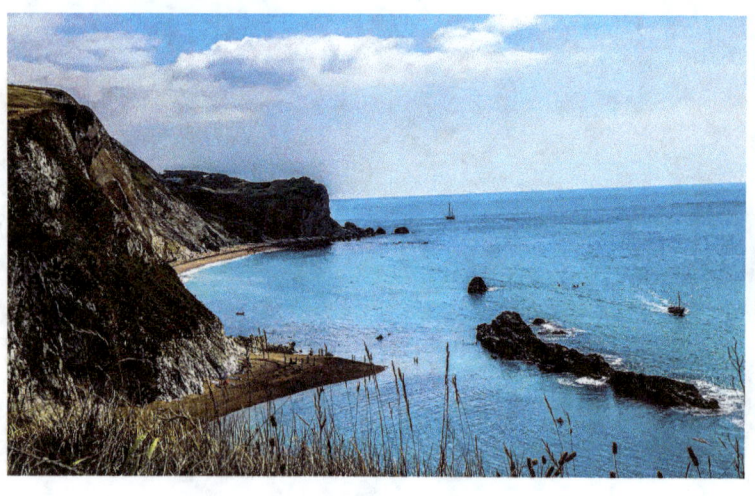

Bedfordshire

Summer day

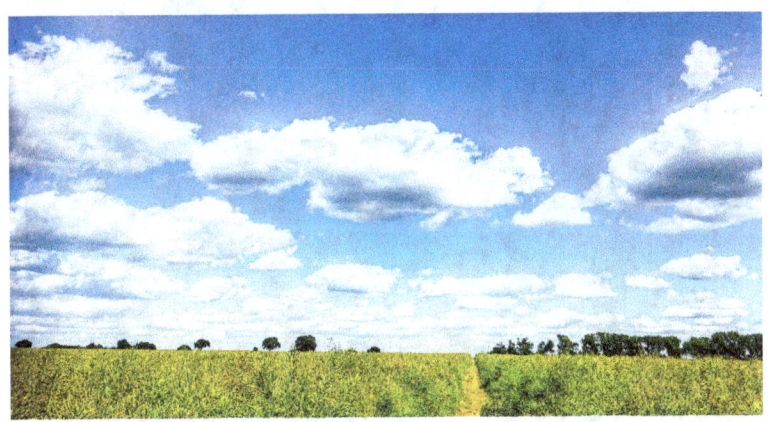

Cambridgeshire

Hinchingbrooke Park

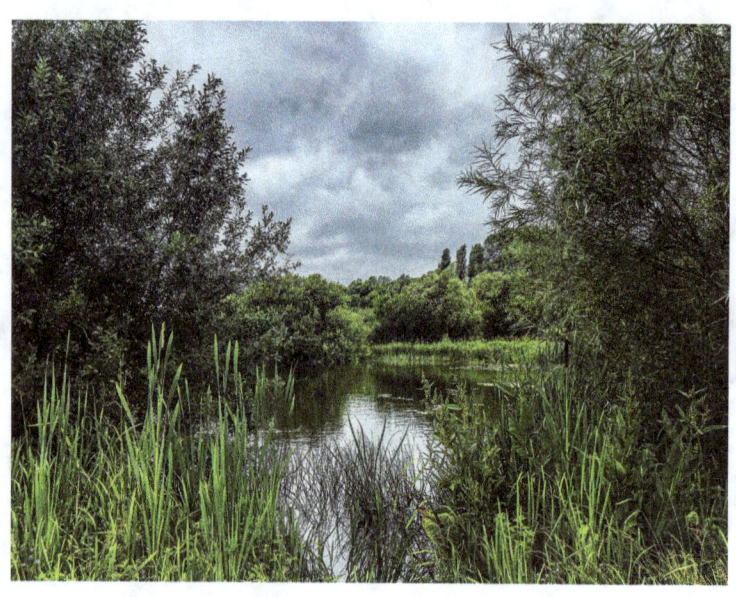

Cornwall

Warm winter day

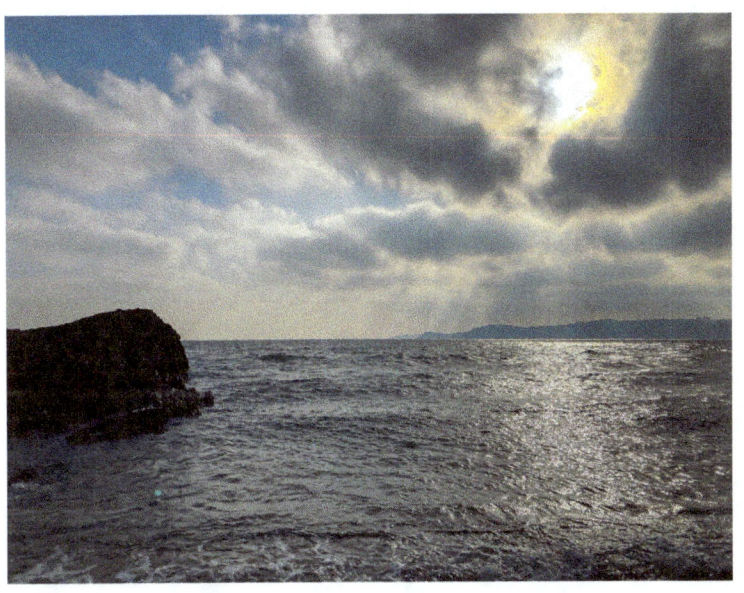

Cornwall

Winter's morning in Looe

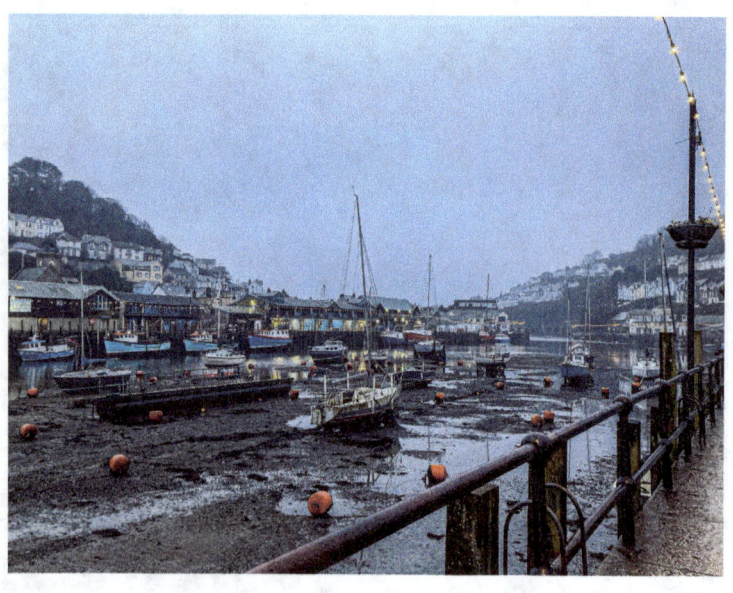

Cornwall

Winter

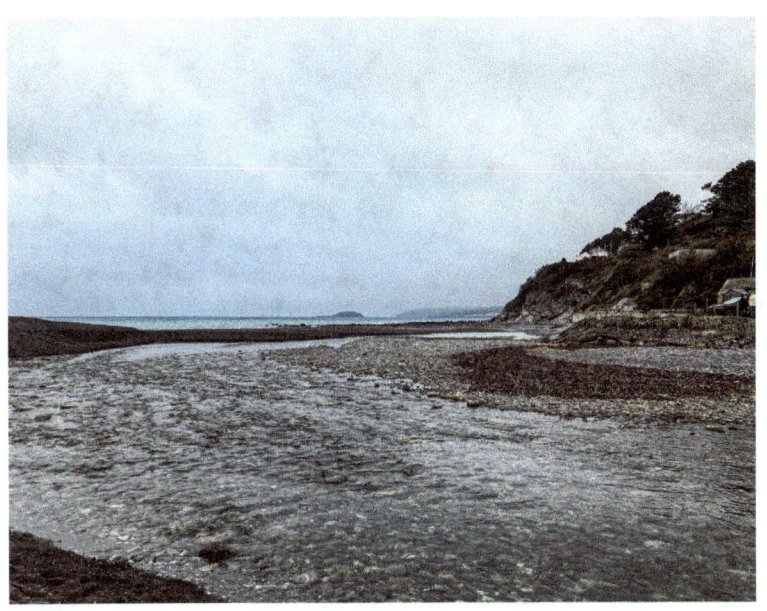

Cambridgeshire

Godmanchester looking towards Portholme

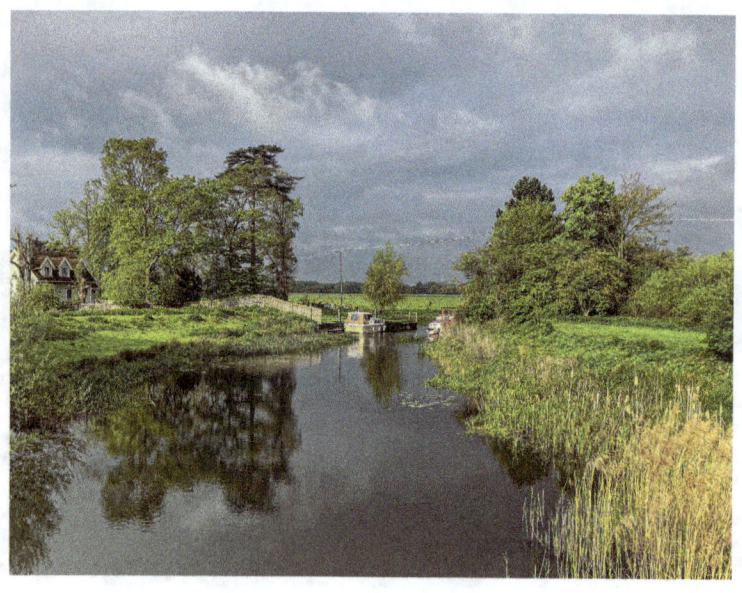

Sussex

Summer day

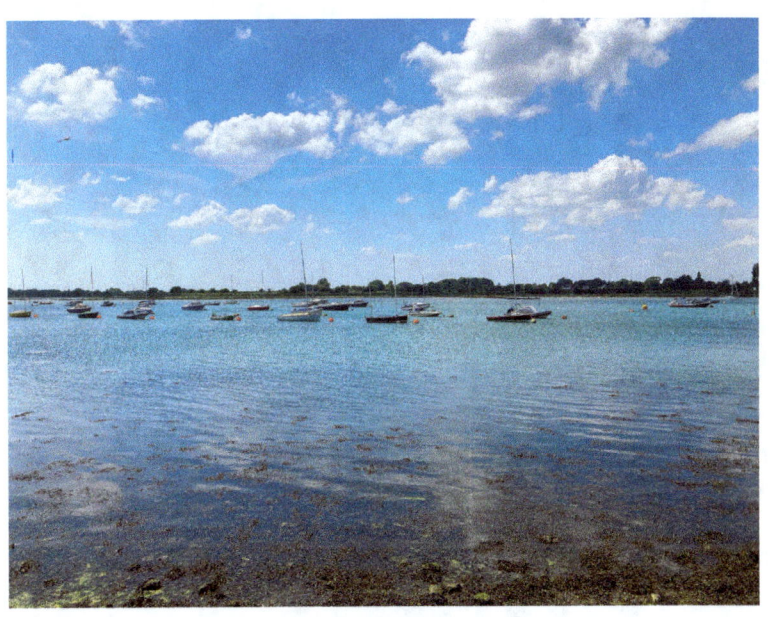

Sussex

Summer day

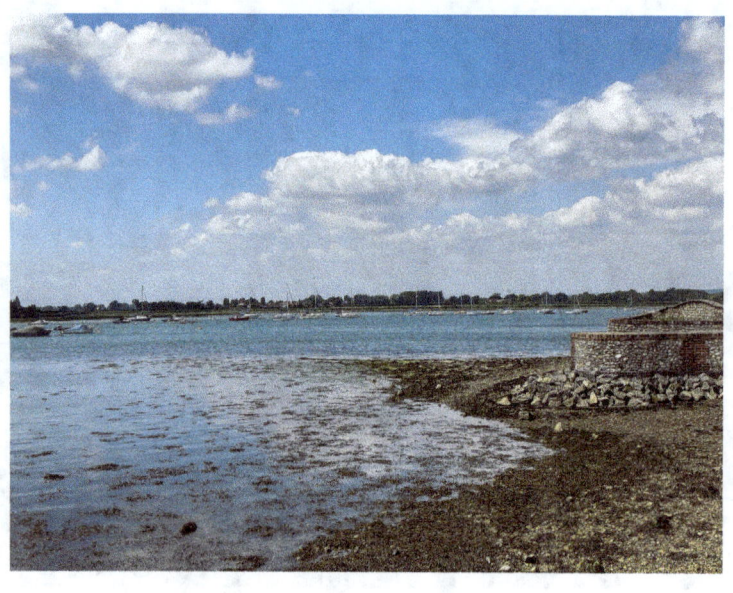

Cambridgeshire

River Ouse Hartford

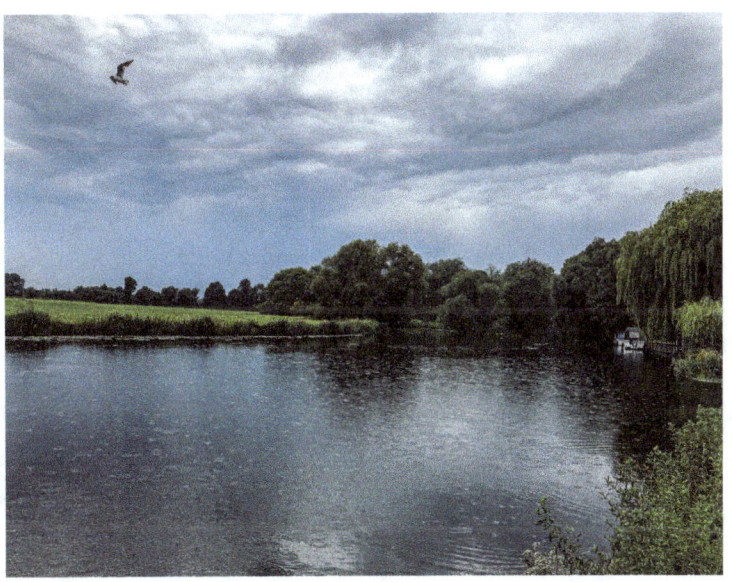

Cambridgeshire

Winter flooded river Ouse

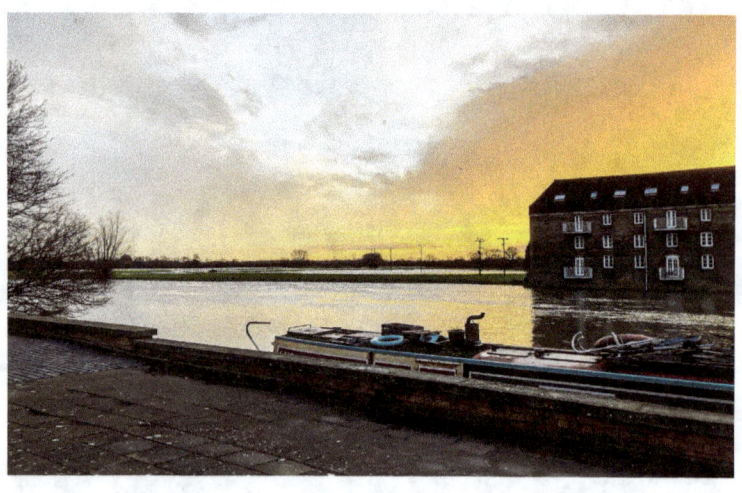

Cambridgeshire

Winter sun over the river Ouse

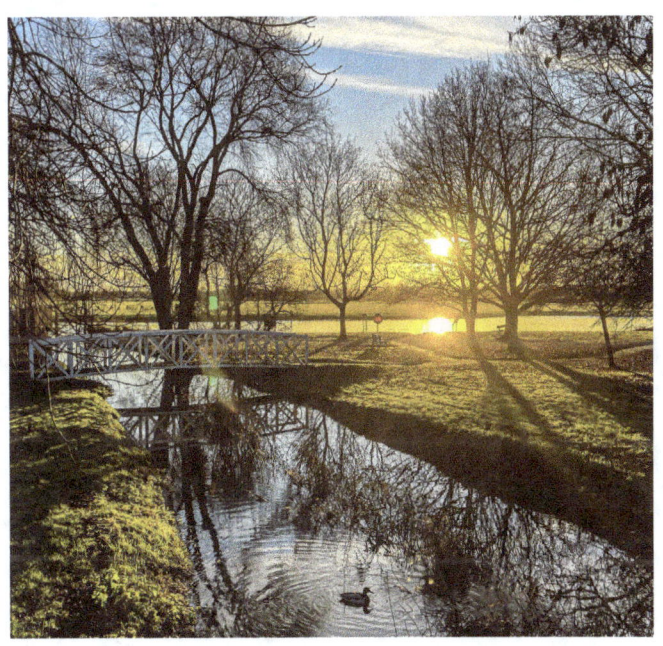

Dorset

Wet summer day in the Poole area

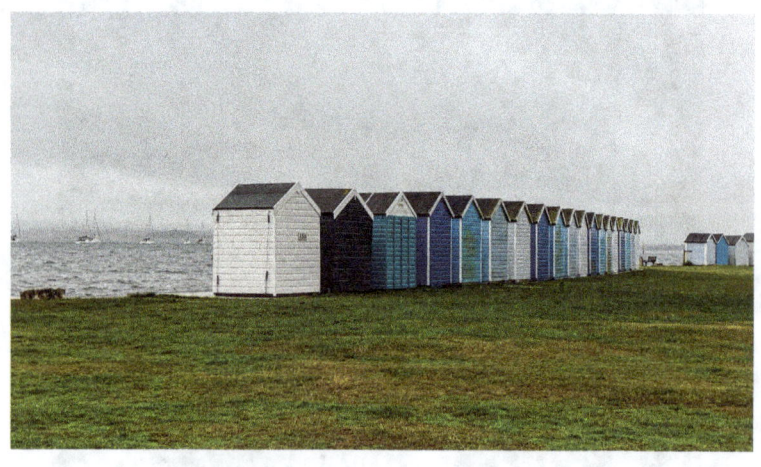

Dorset

Wet summer day in the Poole area

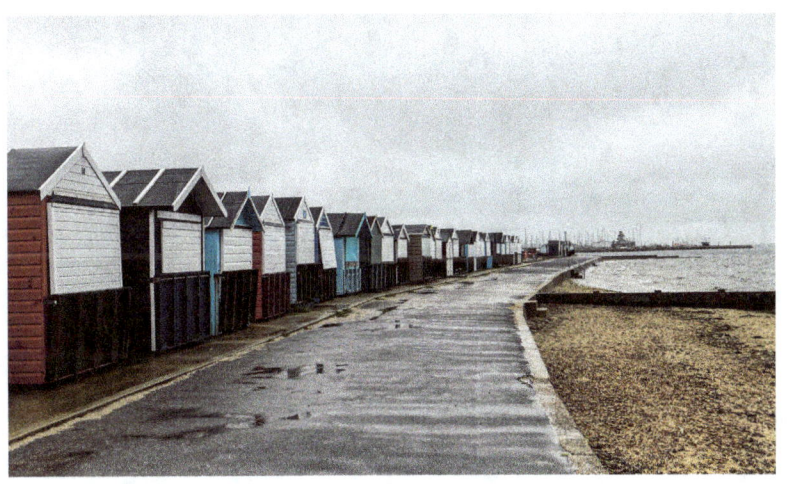

Dorset

Wet morning in Poole

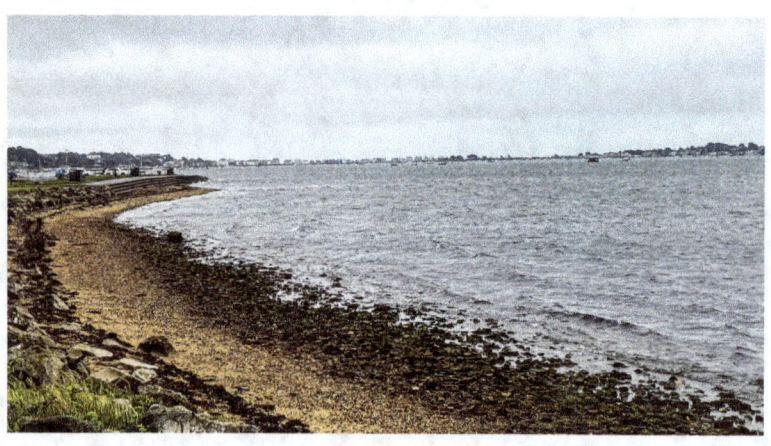

Dorset

Winter sunset in Highcliffe

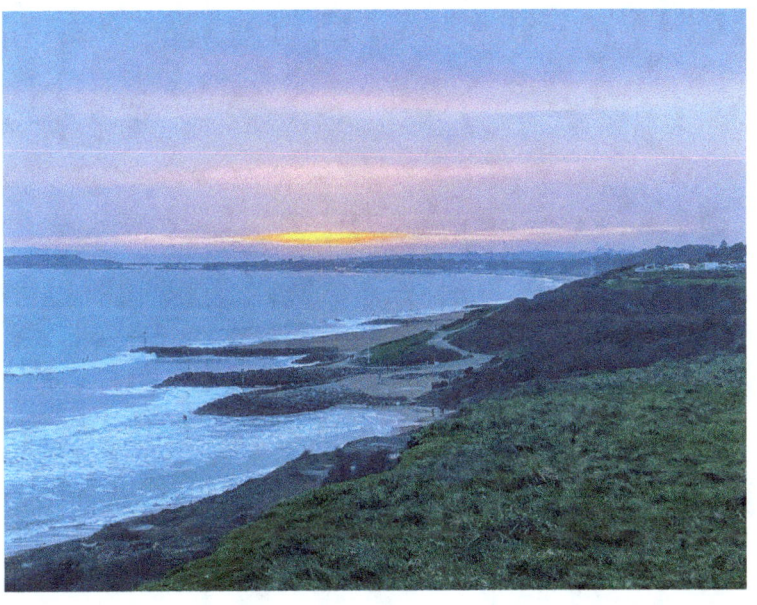

Hampshire

Winter view of the Isle of Wight

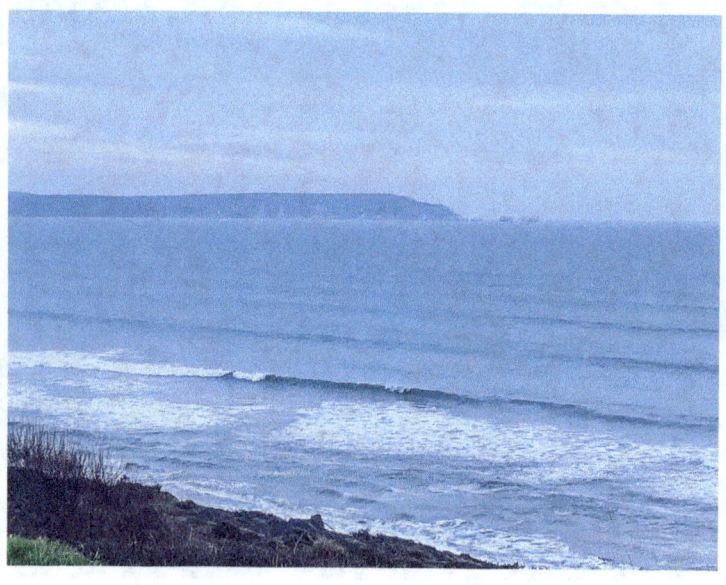

Cambridgeshire

Misting morning on the Ouse

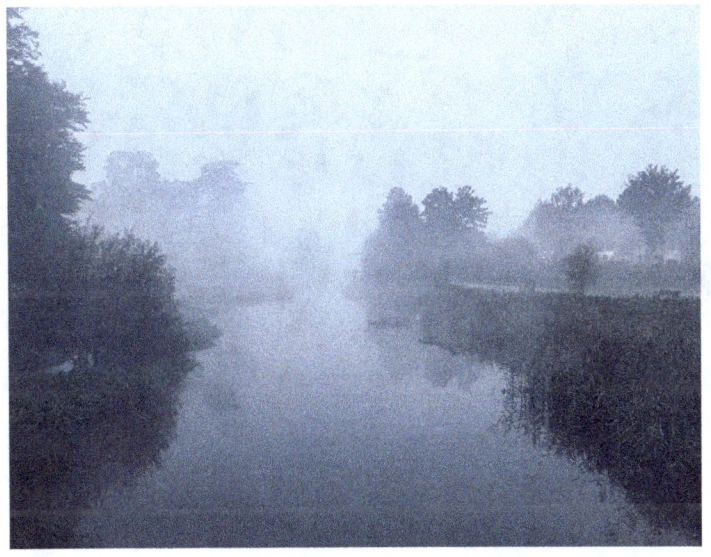

Dorset

Winter view from Mudeford Quay

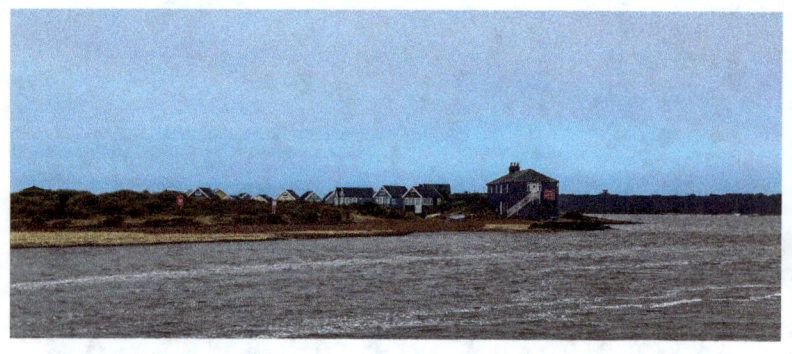